science
essentials

 |  |

The perfect **exam revision** guide

energy and matter

Gerard Cheshire

First published in paperback in 2010 by
Evans Brothers
2a Portman Mansions
Chiltern Street
London W1U 6NR

Series editor:
Harriet Brown

Editor:
Katie Harker

Design:
Robert Walster
Adam Williams

Illustrations:
Peter Bull Art Studio

Printed in China

British Library Cataloguing in
Publication Data

 Cheshire, Gerard, 1965-
   Energy. - (Science essentials.
   Physics)
   1.Force and energy - Juvenile
literature
   I.Title
   531.6

ISBN 9780237541804

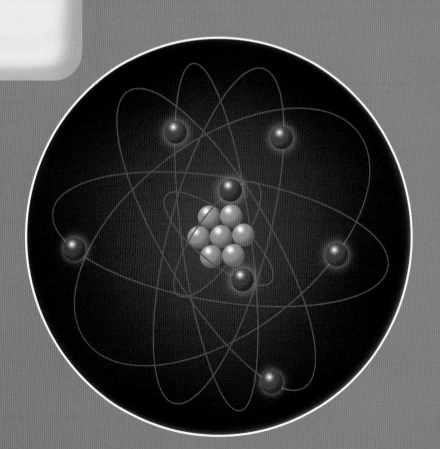

Contents

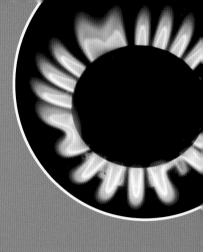

Introduction

We need energy to move, to grow and to carry out important life processes. But energy is all around us, too. Heat energy keeps us warm, light energy

enables us to see the world around us, and sound energy helps us to communicate. Energy is the vital ingredient that causes the changes that we see in our daily lives.

This book takes you on a journey to discover more about the wonderful world of energy and matter. Learn what energy is and how it changes from one form to another. Discover how we use energy sources today, and look at the different ways in which we can save valuable energy for the future. You can also find out about famous scientists, like Antoine Lavoisier and Michael Faraday. Learn how they used their skills to discover what energy is and to develop new machinery to harness the power of energy.

This book also contains feature boxes that will help you to unravel more about the mysteries of sound and vibrations. Test yourself on what you have learnt so far; investigate some of the concepts discussed; find out more key facts; and discover some of the scientific findings of the past and how these might be utilised in the future.

Energy is vital for our survival. Now you can understand more about the power of energy and how it might be used in the future.

DID YOU KNOW?

▶ Watch out for these boxes – they contain surprising and fascinating facts about energy and matter.

TEST YOURSELF

▶ Use these boxes to see how much you've learnt. Try to answer the questions without looking at the book, but take a look if you are really stuck.

INVESTIGATE

▶ These boxes contain experiments that you can carry out at home. The equipment you will need is usually cheap and easy to find.

TIME TRAVEL

▶ These boxes describe scientific discoveries from the past, and fascinating developments that pave the way for the advance of science in the future.

ANSWERS

At the end of this book on page 46, you will find the answers to questions from the 'Test yourself' and 'Investigate' boxes.

GLOSSARY

Words highlighted in **bold** are described in detail in the glossary on pages 46 and 47.

1

What is energy?

Energy is a vital part of our daily lives. The food that we eat gives us the energy we need to move about and to carry out life processes. Plants need energy to grow and reproduce. The machines that we use need energy to carry out their work. Energy is the ingredient that enables things to move, to heat up or to change from one substance into another.

INVISIBLE ENERGY

Energy is invisible – it can't be touched, tasted, heard or smelled. But we can sense the effects that energy has on ourselves or on objects around us. For example, when we feel hot it is because our bodies have too much energy. In order to cool down, we try to get rid of some of this energy. We might remove some clothes so that the energy transfers to cooler air around us, or we might go for a swim to transfer some energy to the cold water. Similarly, when we feel cold it is because our bodies have lost too much energy.

▲ Warm clothes help to prevent energy loss to the cold air.

Putting more clothing on helps to prevent our body warmth from escaping. We can also absorb energy to warm up – by standing next to a fire or having a hot bath, for example. We feel uncomfortable if we get too hot or too cold because our bodies work best within a certain temperature range. Today, energy technology, such as **central heating** and **air conditioning**, helps us to maintain a regular body temperature in areas where it would otherwise be too hot or too cold for us to live comfortably.

◀ A dip in the sea is a good way to cool down on a hot day.

TYPES OF ENERGY

Energy cannot be created or destroyed. Instead it moves from one place to another. As it does so, it often changes from one type of energy into another. The following table summarises the main types of energy:

INVESTIGATE

▶ Write down all the forms of energy that you think you have used today. Where do these energy sources come from?

Energy type	Energy source
(1) Heat (thermal) energy	Hot objects, such as the Sun and fires.
(2) Light energy	Luminous objects such as the Sun, the stars, fires and light bulbs.
(3) Sound energy	Vibrating objects, such as a violin string or your vocal cords.
(4) Electrical energy	The current of an electrical charge.
(5) Kinetic energy	Moving objects.
(6) Potential (stored) energy	Objects with the potential to move, such as a spring or an object that could be pulled by gravity, or a chemical that reacts under certain conditions.
(7) Nuclear energy	The energy that can be released from the nucleus of an atom.

ENERGY SOURCE

The most important source of energy on Earth is the light and heat energy coming from the Sun. The Sun is closest to areas of land around the middle of the Earth (an imaginary line known as the **equator**). These areas are warmed by the Sun's energy. In places half way between the equator and the North or South Pole, the Sun's energy is less intense because it has further to travel. In places near to the North or South Pole the Sun's energy is even weaker so temperatures remain very low. The Earth constantly loses energy to space and the Universe, but it is replaced in equal quantity by the solar **radiation** from the Sun – this helps to keep things in balance.

▼ The Sun has produced energy for billions of years.

▼ The Sun's rays are strongest near to the equator.

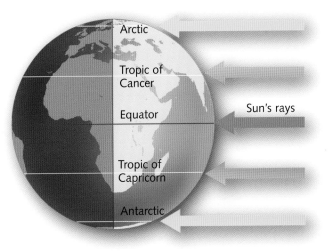

Arctic

Tropic of Cancer

Equator

Sun's rays

Tropic of Capricorn

Antarctic

ENERGY IN THE HOME

In the western world, we use energy in our homes for a variety of reasons – for cooking, lighting, heating, cooling and also for saving ourselves the labour of tasks such as washing clothes, doing the dishes, cleaning and even brushing our teeth. In addition, we use energy to power sources of entertainment and for communication devices. If you look around your home, you'll be amazed at how much energy you use every day.

① HEATING

Keeping our homes warm is important when we live in places that get too cold for us to comfortably maintain our body temperature. The simplest way to produce heat energy is to light a fire, using wood or coal. When the heat produced by these fuels is transferred to the air, the background temperature warms up. In the modern world, central heating systems have now become common. Radiators transfer heat energy into the air using radiation and **convection** (see page 27). Most central heating systems use gas as their energy source, but oil and **electricity** can also be used. Central heating systems usually supply hot water as well.

② COOLING

In hot climates, air conditioning helps to keep temperatures at a comfortable level. Air conditioning units are mostly powered by electricity (although gas can also be used). The units remove heat energy from the air by passing warm air over a cooling system (see page 30). Fridges and freezers also use a cooling system to remove heat energy. Fridges are used to store food at cold temperatures. Freezers are even colder still, and are used to preserve food for months at a time.

③ COOKING

As with heating, the simplest way to cook food or to heat water is to use an open fire. Today, however, we use cookers that are powered by electricity or gas. Some cookers use a combination of fuels, offering an electric oven with a gas hob. Other cooking and food preparation devices (such as microwave ovens, food processors and kettles) are usually powered by electricity.

④ LIGHTING

We use electric lighting to illuminate our world, and to extend the amount of daylight hours in our homes. Light bulbs are powered by electrical energy. **Incandescent** light bulbs are the most common type. When electricity is passed through the light bulb, **friction** causes the filament to heat up and this produces light energy. The problem with incandescent light bulbs is that they produce a lot of heat energy that is wasted. They are gradually being replaced with more energy-efficient bulbs. Fluorescent light bulbs produce light energy in a completely different way. An electrical current is passed through a gas, causing the **atoms** to vibrate and emit energy in the form of light. Fluorescent light bulbs produce less heat so they are a more efficient way to turn electrical energy into light energy.

⑤ CLEANING

Today, we use many electrically-powered devices for washing and cleaning. These include washing machines, tumble driers, dishwashers, vacuum cleaners and personal grooming devices such as electric toothbrushes, electric razors, hair driers and curling tongs. Many of these devices turn electrical energy into kinetic energy or heat energy. Machines of this kind enable us to carry out tasks quickly and efficiently. Without them, these jobs would take a long time.

▲ Some of the most common uses of energy in the home.

⑥ ENTERTAINMENT AND COMMUNICATION

Televisions, radios, music systems and video or dvd players are all entertainment gadgets that have become a part of our daily lives. They change electrical energy into kinetic energy and sound and light energy. These machines are powered by electricity (from the **mains** or from a **battery**). Communication devices, such as computers, telephones and faxes also need electrical energy to work.

⑦ TOOLS

Gardening and maintenance tools are also powered by electricity. They include lawn mowers, hedge trimmers, and tools such as drills, saws and sanders.

2

What is matter?

Matter is a term we use to describe the things that we can see and touch around us. Without matter, nothing could exist in the Universe. All matter, whether it is in the form of a gas, a liquid or a solid, is made from basic building blocks called atoms.

ATOMIC STRUCTURE

Atoms are so small that scientists have yet to look inside one to see its structure. However, atoms are usually represented in drawings that are modelled in a similar way to our Solar System. At the centre there is a **nucleus** (rather like the Sun). This is made from even smaller parts called protons and neutrons. Protons carry a positive electric charge and neutrons carry no electric charge (hence their name which is derived from 'neutral').

AN ATOM

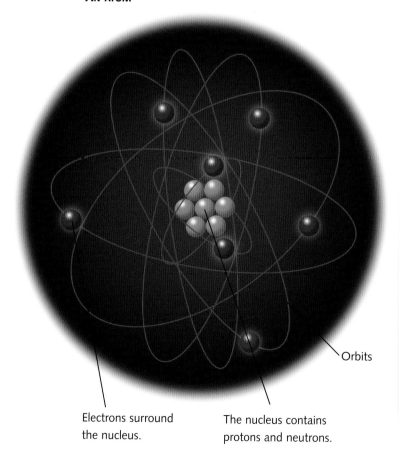

Orbits

Electrons surround the nucleus.

The nucleus contains protons and neutrons.

A cloud of electrons surrounds the nucleus (in a similar way to planets orbiting the Sun). Electrons carry a negative electric charge and are attracted by the positively-charged protons. There are always an equal number of protons and electrons in an atom so that their positive and negative charges are balanced, giving the atom a neutral charge overall.

FORMS OF MATTER

Scientists describe matter in different ways depending on its behaviour. When atoms are fixed together and unable to move, the matter is described as a solid. When atoms are grouped together but are able to move over one another, the matter is described as a liquid. When atoms are free of one another and able to move about, the matter is described as a gas.

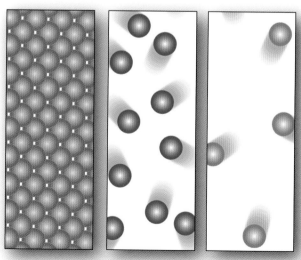

▲ The arrangement of atoms in a solid (left), a liquid (middle) and a gas (right).

Most types of matter can exist as a solid, a liquid or a gas depending on the temperature. When atoms are warmed, they move faster and rebound further when they bump into each other. At low temperatures, atoms have less energy to move, so the matter becomes (or remains) a solid. At warmer temperatures, the atoms have more energy to move, so the matter becomes (or remains) a liquid. At even hotter temperatures, the matter becomes (or remains) a gas. When matter is transformed from a solid to a liquid it is said to be at its **melting point**. When matter changes from a liquid to a solid it is said to be at its **freezing point**. Some liquids, such as oils, become thicker and thicker as

▲ When you boil water in a kettle, some water is released as steam.

temperatures fall. When matter transforms from a liquid to a gas, it is said to be at its boiling point. The reverse is known as its **condensation** point.

▲ Butter is a solid but it melts to a liquid when it is warmed, by a hot crumpet for example.

▲ Condensation on a window is caused by water vapour in the air cooling and turning to water.

ELEMENTS AND COMPOUNDS

An element is a sample of matter that has identical atoms. There are over a hundred types of element, 92 of which occur naturally. Elements can exist in a solid, liquid or gas form. Examples include hydrogen (a gas), aluminium (a solid metal) and mercury (a liquid metal). Elements can change their form when they are cooled or heated. For example, oxygen (O) and hydrogen (H) gas become liquids when they are cooled to very low temperatures. Most elements combine to form **compounds** made up of two or more elements. This can also change their form. Oxygen and hydrogen gas combine to make a compound liquid – water (H_2O), for example.

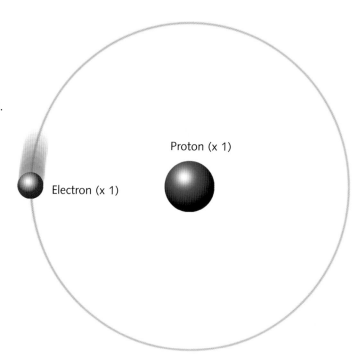

Proton (x 1)

Electron (x 1)

▼ Uranium is the most complex element.

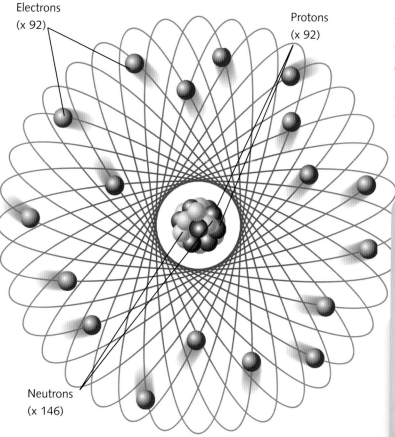

Electrons (x 92)

Protons (x 92)

Neutrons (x 146)

▲ Hydrogen is the simplest element.

The particular structure of an atom determines what element it is. The simplest element is hydrogen (H), whose atoms have just one proton and one electron, with no neutrons. The most complex element is uranium (U), whose atoms contain 92 protons and 92 electrons, with 146 neutrons.

DID YOU KNOW?

▶ The element iodine (I) is unusual because it changes from a solid into a gas when it is heated, without becoming a liquid in between. Iodine gas also changes straight back to a solid when it is cooled.

▶ 'Dry ice' is used for creating smoky effects in clubs or theatres. It is made using frozen carbon dioxide (CO_2) – a compound of carbon and oxygen. The mist is water vapour in the air condensing into visible droplets when it is cooled by the frozen carbon dioxide.

Forms of energy

3

Energy has always existed in one form or another. Although energy cannot be created or destroyed, it can move from one place to another. As it does so, it often changes into a different form. Here we describe the seven main types of energy in the world around us.

HEAT ENERGY

Heat (or thermal) energy is the energy that comes from the movement of atoms in gases, liquids and solids. The temperature of an object is a measure of how much heat energy it has.

A total absence of heat energy would result in all atoms lying perfectly still. We call this temperature 'absolute zero'. It is actually impossible to remove heat energy completely, but scientists have been able to cool material to produce temperatures that are a fraction of a degree above absolute zero.

Heat energy has a tendency to spread out (or dissipate) in the environment. Heat energy causes warm things to cool down and cool things to warm up, so that eventually everything becomes the same temperature. Heat energy is transferred in three ways – conduction (flowing between matter), convection (carried by flowing gases or liquids) and radiation (electromagnetic waves that carry energy through space). We will look at these transfer methods in more detail on pages 26-28.

LIGHT ENERGY

Light is a type of energy that we take for granted every day. Light energy enables us to see the things around us. We see light energy coming from a source, such as a light bulb or the Sun. This type of energy is also called electromagnetic radiation.

▲ The Sun is a major source of light energy. You can see rays of light when the Sun shines through a cloud.

Electrons produce light when they release energy. This light energy travels in waves that vary in length. The light that we see is a small part of the whole range of light waves, which we call the electromagnetic spectrum. The types of light that we cannot see have bigger or smaller wavelengths. We call them different names (such as ultraviolet light or X-rays). The types of light with the smallest wavelength have the greatest energy.

▲ When white light is passed through a glass prism it separates into different wavelengths that we see as colours.

▲ Candles burn wax and air to release heat and light energy.

Light is nature's way of transferring energy through space because light can travel through a vacuum. Light energy travels very fast (almost 300,000 kilometres per second in a vacuum). This means that it takes about two and a half seconds for light to travel from the Earth to the Moon and back again.

Atoms can absorb light energy. A certain wavelength of light energy can cause electrons in an atom to vibrate. The light energy may be immediately released (reflecting the light

energy) or absorbed into the material. In this case the light energy is transferred to heat energy as the movement of atoms causes other atoms to vibrate.

There are two main sources of light – incandescent and luminescent light. Incandescent light comes from things like the Sun, light bulbs or candles, which burn or glow because they are hot. Luminescent light is not caused by heat, but by chemical reactions that cause atoms to vibrate and emit energy in the form of light.

SOUND ENERGY

Sounds are produced when an object vibrates. These vibrations of energy push atoms against one another in pulses, that we call sound waves. The vibrations are then passed from one air particle to the next and eventually reach our ears, where they are translated into a type of signal that the brain can understand. Loud noises have more energy than quiet sounds because the vibrations are bigger. Sounds eventually fade because air particles or other obstacles reflect the energy or absorb it as it passes through. Often the sound energy is converted into heat energy because it causes the atoms in a material to start vibrating.

▲ Our ears convert sound energy into signals that our brain can interpret as different types of noise.

ELECTRICAL ENERGY

Atoms contain a nucleus surrounded by electrons (see page 10). When electrons move from one place to another they carry their negative electric charge with them. The movement of electric charge (or electrons) is called electricity.

Although the electrons of an atom orbit the nucleus in a similar way to the planets that orbit our Sun, their movements are haphazard. Electrons also form into groups that orbit the nucleus at fixed distances, so that they form shells, rather like the layers of an onion. Although atoms need certain numbers of electrons to balance the number of protons, they can also pick up and lose 'free electrons' from their outer shells. When different materials rub together they can transfer electrons. Objects that gain electrons become negatively charged and objects that lose electrons become positively charged. Charged objects have a natural tendency to want to lose their charge and become neutral again. As they do so, they can produce a spark of **static electricity**.

▼ Static electricity is caused by a transfer of electrons.

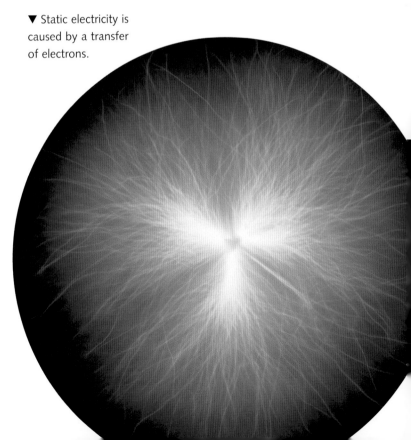

When electrons gather on insulators (materials that do not allow electrons to pass through them) they build up and produce what is called a static charge. When the electrons get a chance to move they do so with a single burst of energy. For example, extra electrons build up around your body because your shoes rub against materials, such as rugs or carpets, when you walk around. The electrons can't move anywhere, but when you touch something metal, such as the handrail of an escalator, they can suddenly move again. The electrons are attracted to the metal and 'leap' towards it, producing a small electric current that you feel as a spark or an electric shock.

An electric current occurs when the electrons are able to flow along a metal wire and their energy is carried with them in a steady stream. Electricity is a convenient way of supplying energy to streets, factories, offices and homes. In most houses, plug sockets are linked to a main power supply. Batteries can also be used for smaller devices. A chemical reaction occurs inside a battery which causes electrons to flow.

▲ This electrical hazard symbol is displayed in areas where electrical wires could cause injury. The body is a good conductor of electricity, which can cause severe burns.

KINETIC ENERGY

When an object is in motion it is said to have kinetic energy. The word 'kinetic' comes from the Greek word for 'to move'. Everything you see moving about you has kinetic energy. Whenever you walk or run, your body has kinetic energy. Machines that move and objects that fall due to the pull of **gravity** have kinetic energy. Kinetic energy can also be passed from one object to another. In a game of football, the player gives kinetic energy to a ball by striking it with his foot. If the ball collides with an obstacle, it will slow down because it has passed some of its energy onto that obstacle. There are many forms of kinetic energy – objects can vibrate or rotate, or they can actually move from one location to another.

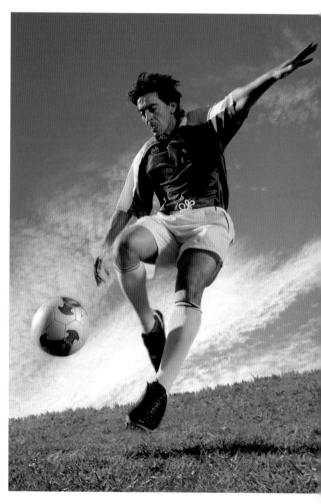

▲ This football gains kinetic energy when it is kicked.

POTENTIAL ENERGY

Matter is said to have potential energy when its energy is not expressed in another form. An object has potential energy before it moves. For example, an object that is prevented from falling has the 'potential' to convert into kinetic energy once it falls. When an object is lifted, its potential energy increases because it is being pulled against the Earth's gravity. If you stretch an elastic band, you give it potential energy. As the elastic band is released, its potential energy is changed to motion.

Sometimes, objects may seem to possess potential energy when this is not the case. For example, when a football is about to be kicked it does not have potential energy. Instead, the kinetic energy from the player's moving leg is quickly transferred to the ball when the foot makes contact. The potential energy actually originates in the muscles of the player's leg before kicking.

Chemical and electrical sources also have potential energy. There are three types of chemical energy – **respiration** (the production of energy in living things), **combustion** (the release of energy from a burning fuel) and **exothermic** chemical reactions (the production of heat during a chemical reaction).

Chemical energy is produced when substances react together. Respiration in humans and animals occurs when food is broken down, using the process of digestion, and some of the components are used to make fuels in the form of sugars and fats. These are used to provide energy for movement and maintaining the warmth needed for the biological processes of life. Humans tend to eat three good meals a day to get the energy they need to keep on the move. Some sources of food provide more energy than others.

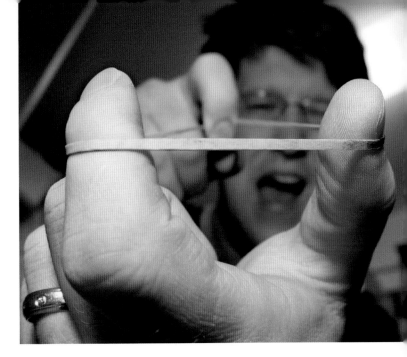

▲ Elastic bands have stored potential energy when they are stretched.

▼ Breakfast cereals are a good source of energy to start the day.

17

▲ Plants make their own food using a process called photosynthesis. Light energy from the Sun is crucial for this process.

Plants use light energy from the Sun to produce sugars from carbon dioxide and water by a process called **photosynthesis**. The sugars are used to provide energy for growth and **reproduction**.

Combustion is when energy is released by burning substances, such as petrol in a car engine or

▲ The heat energy from burning charcoal can cook food.

charcoal on a barbecue. Here, energy is released in the form of heat and light. Exothermic chemical reactions occur when atoms bond together. For example, when plaster of Paris (gypsum) reacts with water it produces heat energy. A battery is another type of chemical reaction. Batteries produce electrical energy (see page 16).

NUCLEAR ENERGY

A huge force holds protons and neutrons together in the nucleus of an atom. This force is a form of potential energy, but to be released the atom must be split apart. When protons and neutrons are separated, they release heat, sound and light energy. This process is known as nuclear fission and is the type of energy made in a nuclear power station. The fuel mostly used is uranium (U), a rare element found in rocks and in seawater. Inside the nuclear power station, uranium atoms are split apart in a controlled **chain reaction**. When the atoms split, particles are released which strike other uranium atoms

▲ Nuclear power plants currently supply around 17 per cent of the world's electricity.

causing them to split, too. In a nuclear power station, control rods are used so that the chain reaction doesn't go too fast, but instead produces a steady flow of energy. The chain reaction gives off heat energy that can be used to boil water and turn machinery to make electricity.

Some countries, such as France, depend on nuclear energy for most of their electricity. Other countries, such as the US and the UK, mainly use coal and oil to make their electrical energy. However, as fossil fuels decline, nuclear energy is becoming a more popular option for the future.

TEST YOURSELF

▶ What types of energy are being used in the following situations?
(1) Switching on a light.
(2) Boiling a kettle.
(3) Playing a CD.
(4) Turning on a torch.
(5) Climbing a ladder.

Nuclear energy can also be produced when atoms join together. In nature, this type of energy is seen in the stars. The Sun, for example, is an enormous mass of hydrogen gas and at the centre, the temperature is over 10 million °C. This heat causes the hydrogen (H) atoms to travel at speeds of around 500 kilometres per second – so fast that when they collide they stick together and form heavier atoms of helium (He). This process, called nuclear fusion, releases enormous amounts of heat and light energy. Nuclear fusion was reproduced on Earth with the invention of the hydrogen bomb, a powerful weapon. In the future, nuclear power stations may use both nuclear fission and fusion to generate energy.

▲ Hydrogen bombs use nuclear fusion to generate enormous amounts of energy.

19

4

Energy sources and resources

There are many potential sources of energy at our disposal. We sometimes refer to them as 'resources' because the energy can be used time and time again. However, this term can be misleading because some energy sources are in danger of running out. To ensure that we have energy supplies for the future, we must continue to look for alternative forms of energy, before it is too late.

FOSSIL FUELS

Fossil fuels are made from the remains of prehistoric plants and animals. They include crude oil, natural gas, coal and peat. Over about 500 million years, dead plants and animals sank deep into the earth or the seabed as they were pushed down by soil and water. Some remains formed rocks as they were squeezed together at high temperatures. Others sank lower down and formed fossil fuels. Fossil fuels are sometimes called 'buried sunshine' because they are made from the remains of plants, that got their energy directly from the Sun via photosynthesis, or animals, that got their energy from eating plants.

Crude oil is a complex mixture of liquid chemicals known as hydrocarbons. These chemicals can be separated by a process called **fractional distillation** and used as fuels to provide energy for a variety of purposes. For example, diesel and petrol are used in the internal combustion engines of vehicles, while paraffin oil is used to heat boilers and as a fuel for jet engines.

Plants decay to form peat. Animal remains sink into the ground.

The peat becomes compressed under layers of soil and forms coal. The oily parts of animals become embedded in the rock.

As the rocks sink they heat up and more oil is produced.

When the rocks become boiling hot, they ooze with light, runny oil. Natural gas is also produced.

▲ Fossil fuels form over millions of years from the remains of dead plants and animals.

▲ Oil rigs are used to drill for oil found under the seabed.

Natural gas is also a mixture of hydrocarbons. It is found near to crude oil reserves. This gaseous fuel includes butane, ethane, methane and propane. Ethane and methane are known as 'dry gases'. We use them as energy supplies for boilers and cookers. Butane and propane are 'wet gases' that can be liquefied under pressure. The liquid gas can then be bottled and used for external applications such as gas-fired barbecues and patio heaters. Both crude oil and natural gas are made from the remains of dead animals.

Coal is a solid fossil fuel made from plant remains. It is often used in an open fire to heat a room. Peat is similar to coal, but has had less time to compact and decompose. It is found nearer the Earth's surface and is sometimes used locally as a fuel for heating homes and for cooking. Coal was once used in vast quantities to provide energy for steam engines. However, today, it is mainly used in power stations to make electricity and in steel-making furnaces. For these purposes, coal has to be refined by heating it in the absence of air to remove any

impurities. Refined coal is called coke, and burns without producing smoke. The impurities are coal tar and coal gas (a mixture of hydrogen and methane). These impurities were once used as a fuel for lighting and heating, but were soon replaced by natural gas which doesn't produce as much smoke.

RENEWABLE FUELS

Other combustible fuels are called renewable fuels, because they are made from plant and animal sources that can be sustained. These 'biomass' fuels include wood, straw, charcoal and dung. We can also obtain and refine fuels from plants and animals, such as animal or vegetable oils and fats. Like fossil fuels, these fuels can be burnt to release energy in the form of heat, light and radiation. The fuels can also be used to power engines and other machinery. Scientists are currently looking at ways to make natural gas from rotting waste material. Methane can be taken from landfill sites where it collects as the rubbish breaks down. The vegetable remains that we throw away can also be turned into gas. Sometimes, we recycle fossil fuels and biomass fuels to make other things. For example, car tyres and plastics are made from refined oil, while paper and cardboard are processed forms of wood fibre. Similarly, old clothing may contain fibres that come from both fossil and biomass fuels.

▲ Coal has been used as an energy source for centuries. It now produces around 37 per cent of the world's electricity.

ENVIRONMENTAL ENERGY

When fossil fuels or biomass fuels are burnt, their energy is released alongside waste products that **pollute** the environment. Some pollutants are obvious, such as smoke and residues that fill the air. Other pollutants are less obvious, but have a far more damaging effect. They include carbon dioxide and methane gas that contribute to the effect of **global warming**, and substances that cause **acid rain** and damage to the ozone layer. To curb the effects of pollutants, scientists are trying to find energy sources that are kinder to the environment.

Wind, waves, tides and rivers are natural expressions of kinetic energy that can be transformed into mechanical and electrical energy with the use of technology. Windmills and waterwheels have existed for hundreds of years, providing mechanical energy for grinding wheat and pumping water. Today, modern versions use the kinetic energy of moving air and water to drive

▲ The strength of the wind can be converted into electrical energy by the turbines of a wind farm.

vanes and turbines attached to generators that produce electricity. Dammed water is used in a similar way to produce hydroelectricity, utilising the kinetic energy released by water as it falls under the force of gravity. Wave and **tidal** power stations also use water to generate electricity (see box p23).

▲ The dam of a hydroelectric power station traps water which then flows through turbines and generators to produce electricity.

THE POWER OF THE SEA

Tidal power is one of the more reliable forms of renewable energy. The tides are dictated by the Moon's orbit around the Earth and occur at regular intervals. Energy from ocean water can be captured in a numbers of ways:

• Wave power station – a machine called an oscillating water column traps air in a large chamber as the waves reach the shoreline. As the waves surge and retract, they fill and empty the chamber with water, pushing and pulling the air in the shaft. The moving air turns a turbine that works a generator, producing electricity.

• Tidal turbine – this device is rather like a windmill. It uses moving water in the sea to turn blades that spin a turbine to generate electricity.

• Pelamis – this device floats on top of the waves and bends with the water's movement. As parts of the device rise and fall, the motion works pumps, which turn a turbine and a generator.

• Tidal barrage (below) – this device stores ocean water behind a barrier until the tide falls. The water from the reserve is then poured slowly through turbines, creating electricity. Alternatively, turbines can be installed directly in the path of the tidal flow. Instead of blocking the water entirely, water flows freely through turbines, creating electricity as the tide moves in and out.

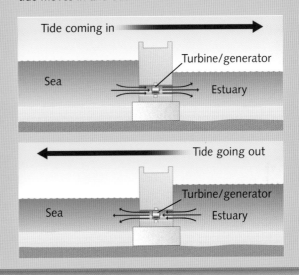

Tide coming in

Turbine/generator

Sea

Estuary

Tide going out

Turbine/generator

Sea

Estuary

SOLAR ENERGY

Solar energy comes in the form of electromagnetic radiation from the Sun. This energy can be transferred into electrical energy thanks to the invention of the solar cell. Some houses are now built with solar panels on the roof (see page 43) that supplement the property's supply of electrical energy. Solar cells absorb the Sun's radiation and release electrons to create an electric current. Sometimes, solar energy is used to heat water circulating in pipes that are painted matt black to absorb as much radiation as possible.

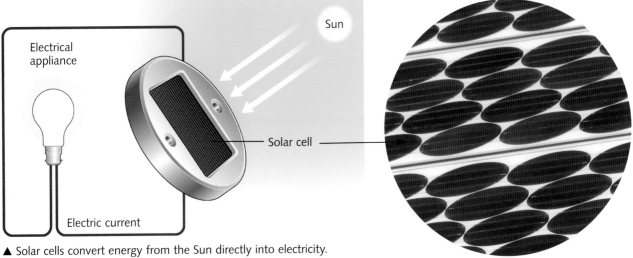

Electrical appliance

Sun

Solar cell

Electric current

▲ Solar cells convert energy from the Sun directly into electricity.

TIME TRAVEL: INTO THE FUTURE

▶ A new device developed by scientists will mean that, in the future, it will be possible to generate electricity from wastewater. The device, called a microbial fuel cell, takes advantage of biological processes that occur naturally in wastewater – such as reactions between partially digested food and bacteria. Fuel cells are devices that, like batteries, generate electricity via chemical reactions. However, unlike batteries that use up substances within the battery to work, fuel cells use external substances, such as hydrogen and oxygen gas, and can continue to work indefinitely as long as the fuel source is readily available.

In a microbial fuel cell, the wastewater is fed through a device that attracts electrons. As bacteria feed on the organic matter in wastewater, they release electrons and protons. The electrons are attracted to the device and flow through a circuit to produce electricity. At the same time the protons combine with oxygen in the air and electrons from the electrical circuit to produce pure water. Scientists believe that if they could capture the electricity in wastewater from 100,000 people, there would be enough energy to power 1,500 homes – and produce clean drinking water at the same time.

THERMAL ENERGY

In some parts of the world, heat energy from the Earth's crust is used to power homes. In Iceland, for example, cold water is pumped into the ground to absorb heat in the rocks. The circulating water becomes very hot and is used to heat homes. In Bath, in the UK, warm water naturally rises to the surface and is used for bathing. The Romans established a settlement here because there was a natural source of hot water that could be used for under-floor heating as well as for bathing. Hot springs also occur in Yellowstone Park in the USA. Here, molten rock is less than five kilometres below the Earth's surface. Yellowstone Park is also home to fumaroles – holes in the ground which spew water vapour and other gases from beneath the Earth's surface.

Changing levels of heat energy in ocean water can also be used to generate electricity. This is called ocean thermal energy conversion (OTEC). OTEC makes use of the difference in temperature between warm surface ocean water and cold water in depths below 600 metres, to turn liquids into gases that can be used to drive turbines and generate electricity.

NUCLEAR POWER

Nuclear power is another source of natural energy because the main fuel that is used (uranium) is found in rocks in the ground. Nuclear energy is made in a power station where uranium atoms are split to release energy (see page 18-19). Nuclear power stations are expensive to build, but once they are set up they are cheap to run because only a small amount of uranium is needed to produce energy. Nuclear energy also doesn't produce the polluting gases that are made when fossil fuels are burnt. However, the waste products from a nuclear power station are radioactive and can be harmful to people and wildlife if they are not safely contained. Radioactive waste remains harmful for thousands of years. It has to be carefully stored in strong metal containers and buried deep underground (or on the ocean floor) to prevent it from contaminating the environment.

TEST YOURSELF

▶ How many fossil fuels can you name? What are they made from? What are they used for?

Energy transfer

When energy changes from one form to another, it does so in different ways. Sometimes, the same type of energy moves from one object to another. This is known as direct transfer. At other times, one form of energy converts into another. We call this indirect transfer.

5

LAWS OF CONSERVATION

The Universe has always contained a set amount of energy and it will continue to contain this energy forever. In a similar way, the Universe has contained (and always will contain) the same amount of matter. Although atoms can be destroyed, the particles from which they are made always recombine in one way or another. This is known as the 'Law of Conservation of Mass' and was formulated by the French chemist Antoine Lavoisier in 1774. Because energy can't be created or destroyed, it has to come from somewhere and it always needs somewhere to go to. This is known as the 'Law of Conservation of Energy' and was formulated by the German physicist Hermann von Helmholtz in 1847.

DIRECT TRANSFER

An example of direct transfer is when heat energy flows from one object to another. This can happen in three ways – conduction, convection and radiation. When we talk about objects heating up or cooling down we are actually describing the amount of energy held within the atoms of the object. When atoms gather more energy, their electrons move about

◀ Antoine Lavoisier

more vigorously. The object also increases in temperature and expands because the atoms grow larger in size. Similarly, when atoms lose energy their electrons begin to move about more slowly. The object contracts when there is less energy because the atoms grow smaller in size as they cool down.

▼ This bridge has a joint made of interlocking metal teeth. If the bridge expands in the heat of the Sun, the teeth move together. This prevents the bridge from buckling and keeps the road surface smooth.

When there are extreme changes in energy levels, the characteristics or qualities of a material will change dramatically. For example, water with very little energy freezes into ice. As it gains energy it melts into liquid water. If its energy levels continue to rise, it expands and becomes lighter than cool water. Eventually the atoms move so vigorously that the water boils and turns into steam or water vapour.

▲ The atoms in an iceberg have very little energy.

▲ The atoms in this huge steam cloud have lots of energy. The steam comes from boiling ocean water that has been heated by molten lava from the Kilauea volcano in Hawaii.

INVESTIGATE

▶ Take ten ice cubes out of the freezer and place them in a saucepan. Heat them over a gentle heat. Watch as the ice melts to form water. Then watch as the water boils to form steam. Can you draw a picture to show how the arrangement of atoms changes in each case?

CONDUCTION

Conduction is the way in which heat is transferred through a material by moving particles. Conduction happens when two objects at different temperatures come into contact. Heat energy flows from warmer to cooler objects until they are both at the same temperature (see page 13). When the objects touch, the faster moving atoms of the warmer object collide with the slow-moving atoms of the cold object. As the atoms collide, the warmer atoms transfer some of their energy. As the slow-moving atoms warm up they move faster and collide with other slow-moving atoms, causing these to warm up, too.

When you cook in a saucepan, the heat of the cooker's electric rings, or gas flames, causes the atoms on the bottom of the saucepan to vibrate. These moving atoms transfer their energy to colder atoms nearby which are also made to vibrate. Eventually all of the atoms in the bottom of the pan vibrate and the saucepan heats up. Materials that transfer heat well (such as metals) are called conductors, while materials that do not transfer heat well (such as wood and plastic) are called insulators. Saucepan handles are often covered with plastic. As a good insulator, the plastic stops the handle from becoming too warm to touch. Solids are better conductors than liquids and liquids are better conductor than gases. This is because energy is transferred faster if the atoms are closer together.

CONVECTION

Convection is the movement of gases or liquids from a cooler area to a warmer area. Convection happens because gases and liquids change in density as they heat up. Convection is what causes pasta shapes to rise and fall in a pot of heating water. The warmer areas of water are less dense and therefore rise, pushing the pasta up. Meanwhile, the cooler parts of the water fall because they are denser, allowing the pasta to fall.

Convection currents also occur in the oceans as the surface of the water nearest to the equator is warmed by the heat of the Sun (see page 7) and moves towards the North and South Poles where the water is colder. This movement forces colder water to move towards the Equator and helps to regulate the Earth's climate.

▲ A gas flame heats this saucepan by conduction. The heat is then transferred to the water which rises and falls with convection currents as it becomes more and less dense. The flow of water also moves the pasta shapes around.

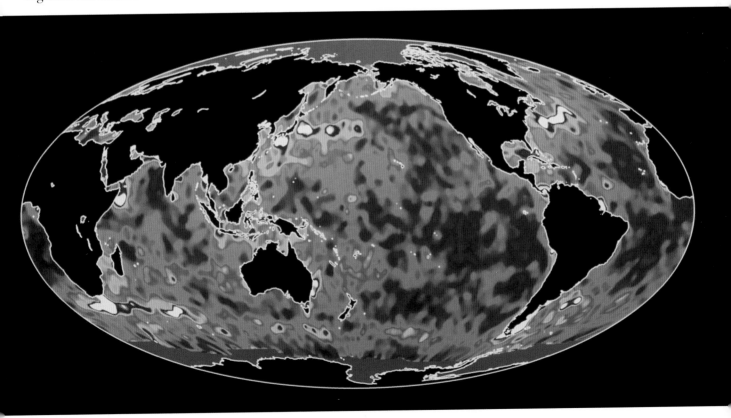

▲ This satellite map shows the world's major ocean convection currents (in yellow, red and white). Without the Gulf Stream (off North America, top right), the UK and other places in Europe would be as cold as Canada, at the same latitude. Other major ocean currents include the Agulhas Current (south of Africa, bottom left) and the Kuroshio Current (off Japan, upper centre).

Convection currents occur in the air, too. When a radiator warms a room, the air above the radiator rises and is replaced by cooler air. This cycle repeats as the room warms up. Warm air is lighter than cold air and so it rises, and is replaced by the cooler air that falls. A similar movement of air causes the wind to blow.

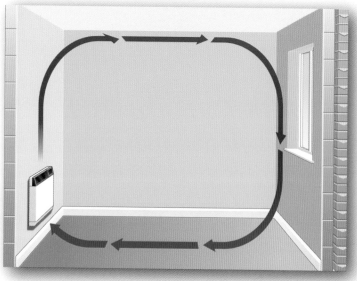

▲ This radiator is on one side of the room, but convection currents of air mean that the whole room warms up.

RADIATION

Radiation is caused by electromagnetic waves that transfer heat directly through space. An example of radiation is the heat of the Sun. The Sun's energy cannot reach us by conduction or convection because there are no solids, liquids or gases to transfer this energy through space. Instead, the Sun's heat and light energy travels in straight lines (or rays) of radiation. The transfer of heat by radiation travels at the speed of light and covers great distances, even in a vacuum.

Heat transferred through radiation can be absorbed or reflected. Cold-blooded animals use heat radiation from the Sun to warm themselves. Some materials absorb heat radiation better than others. The ability of the Earth to absorb the heat from the Sun means that the Earth stays relatively warm at night when the Sun isn't shining. Dark surfaces absorb more heat than light surfaces. You stay cooler in the summer if you wear light-coloured clothes.

▼ Lizards are cold-blooded animals. They have to use the energy of the Sun to warm themselves up.

INDIRECT TRANSFER

When energy changes from one form to another it is called indirect transfer. Energy changes all the time. When we rub our hands together vigorously, our palms become hot. This is because the kinetic energy from our moving hands is converted into heat energy caused by friction. When a firework rocket is set alight, chemical energy converts into the kinetic energy of the rocket's motion and a considerable amount of light, sound and heat energy when the rocket explodes.

When we move around, our body transfers the chemical energy from the food that we eat, into kinetic energy. Some of the chemical energy also converts into heat energy, so that we warm up. When an object falls, its potential energy is lost as it gains kinetic energy. The potential energy from a battery is converted into electrical energy that can be used to work machinery. In today's world we use many devices to help us to change energy from one form into another (see chapter 7).

▼ We have the energy to move around because the chemical energy from the food that we eat can be converted into kinetic energy.

▲ The chemical energy in a firework is released as kinetic, heat, sound and light energy.

DID YOU KNOW?

▶ You experience heat transfer by conduction whenever you touch something that is hotter or colder than your skin, for example, when you wash your hands in warm or cold water. When you climb into a hot bath the heat energy of the water transfers to your body so that your temperature rises while that of the water lowers.

▶ Metals tend to feel cold but they are not really colder than our hands. Metals feel cold because they conduct heat away from our hands. We perceive this heat loss as coldness.

REMOVING HEAT ENERGY

In our modern homes we use energy to perform different tasks, such as heating, cooking and powering electronic devices (see pages 8-9). Energy naturally makes things warmer, but by removing energy we can also make things colder. Fridges, freezers and air conditioning units are used to remove energy to keep our food and drinks cold or to cool the air in a room.

To understand how cooling devices work it is useful to look at an analogy of a bicycle pump. If you block the hose of a bicycle pump and push the handle forwards, the air inside gets compressed as it is squeezed into a small space. The air also becomes warmer because the kinetic energy of your moving arm is transferred to the air **molecules** which are forced to move faster, within a confined space.

If the air in the bicycle pump is held so that it remains compressed, the heat will eventually escape (dissipate) from the pump so that the compressed air cools down to room temperature. If the cool compressed air is now made to expand, by pulling the handle backwards, it causes the surrounding air to become colder. This is because the air molecules in the pump have very little energy to share between them, so they start absorbing energy from the surrounding air in the room, making it feel colder.

This is the principle by which cooling devices, such as fridges, freezers and air conditioning units, operate. Instead of using air, these devices use

▶ We use fridges to keep our food cool so that it stays fresh for longer.

special chemicals, called volatile fluids, which are pumped to circulate through pipes of varying size. When volatile fluids flow through the pipes of a fridge, they move from an area of high pressure to an area of low pressure. This causes the liquid to expand and eventually evaporate into a gas. As the liquid evaporates it absorbs heat, making the inside of the fridge colder. The gas is then compressed so that it cools and condenses into a liquid and the cycle then begins all over again. Air conditioning units work in much the same way, to remove heat energy from the air in a warm room.

▶ We use three different temperature scales today, two of which are based on the behaviour of water. In 1724, German scientist Gabriel Fahrenheit invented the Fahrenheit (°F) scale. Fahrenheit set 0°F as the coldest temperature that he could achieve in his laboratory and 100°F as his own body temperature. His scale was divided into 96 divisions that gave 32°F as the freezing/melting point of water and 212°F as the boiling/condensing point of water.

Two decades later, in 1742, the Swedish physicist Anders Celsius invented the Celsius (°C) scale. This scale has 0°C as the freezing/melting point of water and 100°C as the boiling/condensing point of water. The Celsius scale is also known as the Centigrade scale (centigrade means 'consisting of or divided into 100 degrees').

In 1848, the Scottish physicist, Lord William Thomson Kelvin took the process one step further when he invented the Kelvin scale. This scale is the same as the Celsius scale except that its zero point is –273°C, the coldest temperature theoretically possible. We call this temperature 'absolute zero' (see page 13).

Today, scientists use the Kelvin scale, although the Celsius scale is popular in everyday life. The Fahrenheit

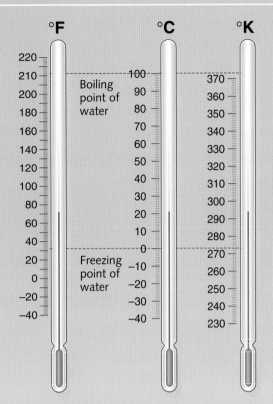

▲ **These thermometers compare readings of the three temperature scales.**

scale is also still used, particularly for recording the weather. There are almost two fahrenheit degrees for every celsius degree, giving a more specific measurement.

◀ **Anders Celsius**

Lord William ▶
Thomson Kelvin

6

Storing energy

Sometimes, energy is stored before it is transferred. An energy source that is not in use is said to have potential energy. Potential energy is found in all the things around us that have the potential to move. Substances that can react together chemically have potential energy, too. Some of the most useful sources of stored energy that we have discovered are the fossil fuels that we burn to produce energy to power things in our homes, our schools and our factories.

THE FOOD OF LIFE

Humans, animals and plants store their potential energy in the form of carbohydrates (sugars and starches) and fats. Humans and animals get this energy from the food that they eat, and plants get energy from the sunlight that they convert in a process called photosynthesis. In each case, chemical reactions occur to release the energy so that it can be used for growing, moving and keeping the organism alive.

MACHINE POWER

Stored energy can be found in the machines that we use to do work for us. For example, clocks and watches have the potential energy of wound up springs which power the mechanical process that records time passing. When the springs are wound up they store potential energy because they are elastic and try to unwind. Small clocks have a mechanism that controls the rate at which the springs move. A grandfather clock uses weights instead of springs. These weights are attached to ropes or chains and have potential energy that transfers to kinetic energy when they pull down on the ropes. A pendulum is used to control the speed at which the weights fall. Every now and then, the weights need to be reset by turning a wheel that lifts them back up again so that they have more potential energy. Modern clocks are powered with batteries, but even these have potential energy stored inside the chemicals of the batteries.

▶ A watch can keep time because it uses the potential energy of wound up springs.

INSTANT ENERGY

Some fuels, such as wood and natural gas, have stored energy that we can use directly to turn into heat and light energy. Today, natural gas is commonly used in homes for cooking and to heat water for baths and radiators. Wood is another fuel that can be used directly. Before electricity was invented a wood fire was a common source of energy to heat homes and to cook food.

In the modern world, most of the energy that we now use comes in the form of electricity or electrical energy. Electricity is a convenient form of energy. It is produced in power stations but a network of power lines transports the energy to our homes to be used whenever it is needed.

▼ A grid of power lines can connect an entire country to a supply of electrical energy.

▲ When we burn natural gas it gives off a lot of heat energy. This can be used to cook food and to heat the water and central heating systems in our homes.

Electricity comes from power stations that use a variety of potential energy sources to drive their generators. The majority of power stations burn combustible fuels such as coal and oil to heat water into steam. The steam drives turbines – giant rotating shafts. These, in turn, work generators that move electric conductors through magnetic fields. The motion of these conductors cutting across a magnetic field forces electrons in the conductors to move, creating electrical currents.

DID YOU KNOW?

▶ The hydrocarbons that make up natural gas are all odourless. To make them safer to use, a chemical is added, so that gas leaks can be detected by smell. This chemical – known as methanethiol or methyl mercaptan – occurs naturally. It smells a bit like rotten eggs.

Some power stations release potential energy by burning a fuel, such as coal, oil or gas. However, this method produces polluting gases that have been found to harm the environment. In recent years, other types of power station have been developed that use a different form of potential energy. Hydroelectric power stations for example (see page 22), use the potential energy of water that is stored in a dam. When this water falls, it releases the energy in the form of kinetic energy that can be converted into electrical energy using turbines and generators. Nuclear power stations use the potential energy stored within an atom to heat water that can drive turbines and a generator. Nuclear power can heat water without the need for burning and is considered to be a 'cleaner' fuel for this reason.

◀ When water falls from a height it releases a tremendous force that can be used to generate electricity.

DID YOU KNOW?

▶ Although we know the boiling point of water as 100°C, this measurement is only true at sea level. The temperature at which water boils increases below sea level and decreases above sea level because of the changing density of the air molecules. Below sea level the air is denser, so water needs more energy to escape as a gas. Above sea level the air is less dense, so the water requires less energy to escape. A pressure cooker takes advantage of this fact. The air-tight lid increases the pressure inside the pan causing water to boil at a temperature higher than 100°C. This means that food can be cooked at higher temperatures, very quickly. In effect, the pressure cooker 'stores' energy so that it becomes concentrated in a small area. This historical artwork shows one of the first pressure cookers, invented in 1679. The iron pot has a sealed lid and a pressure vent (upper centre) that allows steam to escape and stops the pot from exploding.

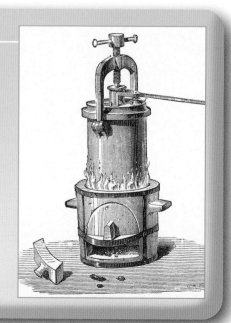

Energy transfer devices

7

Sometimes, there are limited uses to the energy that is transferred from potential energy sources. For example, when fuels are burnt, the heat and light energy is useful for lighting, cooking and heating, but that is all. Luckily, we have now found ways to convert energy into more useful energy types. The devices that have been invented for these purposes have transformed the way in which we use energy in our daily lives.

CONVERTING ENERGY OURSELVES

Humans (and animals) convert non-useful energy into useful energy, every day. To move our bodies and limbs we have to convert chemical energy into mechanical energy. Humans have learnt to apply this mechanical energy for other means – to operate the controls of a car or a computer game, for example. Whether we turn the handle of a door, prepare a sandwich or make a cup of coffee, our actions require us to generate useful energy for it to happen at all. The food that we eat is the fuel for the energy that we need.

ENERGY AND WILDLIFE

Fires can be very damaging but animals and plants sometimes take advantage of the energy released by combustion when it occurs naturally, due to lightning striking the ground. Some trees for example, require a good scorching with fire for their seeds to be released and to germinate. Young trees have a better chance of establishing themselves when a fire has cleared an area of pests or predators. Some trees have actually evolved to keep their seeds until conditions are well suited to them – such as after a fire.

▼ The energy of a forest fire can be lethal, but some plants have adapted to make the most of these conditions.

▲ Vertical convection currents – called thermals – help this Andean Condor to fly upwards and downwards.

Many species take advantage of the kinetic energy in moving air and water. This kinetic energy is generated by thermal energy, causing convection currents. Birds and insects, for example, use the rising air of convection currents when they fly. On a larger scale, some animals use major currents to migrate over large distances through the skies and oceans. In the oceans, marine animals swim great distances with the aid of convection currents. Animals such as plankton and fish also take advantage of this kinetic energy, which transports food through the water without them having to move.

Plants are well known for their ability to capture the energy of solar radiation by the process of photosynthesis, helping them to make their food. Animals too, absorb solar radiation to provide themselves with energy. Cold-blooded animals often bask in the Sun to warm their muscles and their blood (see page 28). On land and in the oceans, colonies of simple plants and animals have been found in places where thermal heat escapes from the Earth's crust. These plants and animals rely on the warmth to survive.

▶ Butterflies often sit with their wings open. Their wings act as solar panels, gathering heat energy from the Sun to warm them.

USING ENERGY FOR TRANSPORTATION

The vehicles that we use to transport us from place to place use clever energy transfer devices to make the most of the fuel that they use. Early steam trains are a good example of a simple way to transfer non-useful energy into useful energy. When coal is burnt in the train's engine, the energy released is used to boil water to produce steam. This steam is then used to drive pistons that, in turn, push and pull piston rods that cause other parts of the machinery to rotate. By simply burning coal, potential energy has been transferred into heat energy that causes machinery to move (kinetic energy). Steam trains are rarely used today, however, because the burning of coal releases polluting gases into the atmosphere.

Power stations use the same principles as a steam train, except that the steam is used to drive steam turbines attached to generators, which produce electricity. Coal, gas or oil are burnt to produce the heat that boils water. Today, power stations are still polluting, but companies take special measures to filter the gases that are released during the burning process. This helps to reduce the impact that a power station has on the environment.

Engines and motors work in a similar way to a steam engine. Internal combustion engines are used in a variety of modern vehicles, from cars to trains. These engines use the energy from ignited petrol or diesel to push pistons. In aeroplanes, jet engines use the energy from aviation fuel to operate moving parts.

▲ Steam trains convert the potential energy in coal into kinetic energy, to move a locomotive.

◄ Coal, oil and gas power stations produce steam from boiling water to turn turbines that are attached to generators to make electricity.

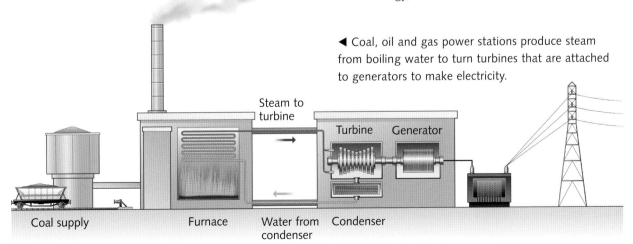

Coal supply   Furnace   Water from condenser   Condenser

Steam to turbine

Turbine   Generator

THE POWER OF ELECTRICITY

Electricity is not a useful energy in itself, but it can be transferred into extremely useful forms of energy. Motors use an electromagnetic force to convert electricity into kinetic energy that can be used to turn machinery. In our homes, electricity can also be used to make light, heat and sound energy (see pages 8-9). Today, it would be hard to imagine a world without electricity. Sometimes, there is a problem with the electrical power supply and many systems that we have come to rely on are unable to work. At these times, the power of electricity becomes very apparent. How many electrical appliances have you used today? What would you have been unable to do without the use of electricity?

▼ The computer is perhaps the single most important device in our modern lives, that converts electrical energy into useful energy.

ENERGY LOSS

Whenever one form of energy is transferred to another, a certain amount of energy is lost to the environment. The ratio between the amounts of energy transferred and lost is known as the transfer efficiency. For example, when a fuel is burnt it is only ever possible to convert about 40 per cent of the potential energy to useful energy, such as electricity. This means that at least 60 per cent will be lost. The more often an energy source is transferred, the more energy is lost to the environment each time. For example, if a motor then uses the electricity, a further 60 per cent of the remaining 40 per cent of energy will be lost. This means that a total of 84 per cent of the original energy has been lost along the way. Manufacturers of machinery are continually looking at ways to minimise the amount of energy that is lost when energy is transferred.

ENERGY LOSS AND INSULATION

When energy from one isolated system escapes to another the process is called energy loss. One way to minimise energy loss is by insulation – providing a barrier that attempts to prevent the passage of energy from one place to another. For example, a thermos flask is used to keep hot drinks hot or cold drinks cold. It works because it has a double skin between which there is a vacuum. A vacuum is very good at insulating the passage of heat energy because there are no air molecules for energy to travel through using conduction or convection (see pages 26-27). However, a flask doesn't prevent heat energy from filling the gap, so eventually the temperature of the drink balances out with the temperature in the outside environment. A vacuum is also effective at preventing energy from escaping in the form of sound waves, which is why double glazing is good for keeping warmth in and noise out, while also letting light and radiation through.

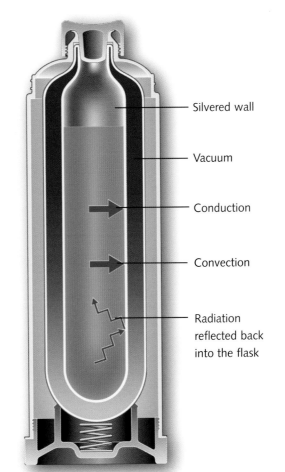

- Silvered wall

- Vacuum

- Conduction

- Convection

- Radiation reflected back into the flask

▲ A thermos flask uses a vacuum to insulate a container so that drinks remain hot or cold for longer.

DID YOU KNOW?

▶ When insects fly they flap their wings up to 1,000 times per second. This uses about 100 times more energy than they need at rest – energy that would be impossible to produce by respiration alone. Scientists believe that in order to generate this kind of energy, insects use elastic mechanisms on their body to reduce energy consumption. At the end of each wing stroke an elastic mechanism (or 'wing hinge') is stretched and this stores some of the energy that is then used as the mechanism recoils for the start of the next wing stroke. Birds are also thought to use a similar mechanism to conserve energy. Hummingbirds, for example (right), beat their wings up to 80 times a second.

Most of us use electricity every day in our lives and we now take this form of energy for granted. But electricity has only been available for domestic use since the early part of the 1900s. Electricity was often regarded with suspicion and its potential was never fully realised, until the end of the 1800s.

The rise of electricity

In the 1800s, electricity began to be developed as an energy supply for industrial use. However, at this time, electricity was something that scientists played around with and experimented with, without realising its potential. Sometimes, electricity was used purely as a source of entertainment – scientists and showmen alike would perform electrical experiments in front of paying audiences as an alternative to theatre, opera or music hall shows. Even when the potential of electricity began to be realised, electricity was blighted by its reputation for being dangerous and unpredictable to use. Because the workings of electricity weren't easily understood (compared to other fuel sources such as burning wood, coal or gas) it was believed to possess mysterious, even magical qualities.

▲ Alessandro Volta

The story of electricity's rise to greatness began in 1799, when the work of two Italian scientists, Alessandro Volta and Luigi Galvani, led to the invention of the first electric cell or battery – the Voltaic pile. During his work, Galvani noticed that dissected frogs' legs would jump if they were hung from a copper wire. After further investigations, Volta discovered that if he hung the copper wire from an iron bar, electricity was produced. Galvani and Volta had made a simple electrical (or 'voltaic') cell – it was actually electricity that had made the frogs' legs twitch! This discovery showed that if two metal wires touch in water, one metal dissolves in a chemical reaction that drives electricity around the wire circuit. This invention encouraged other scientists to experiment with current electricity for the first time.

Over the next 30 years, various scientists began to discover more about how and why electricity behaves in the way it does. Then, in 1831, the British scientist Michael Faraday and the American scientist Joseph Henry, invented the electric motor, the dynamo and the transformer. As soon as practical versions of these devices were developed, electricity became an accepted alternative to traditional energy forms, such as steam power and gas lighting. The devices also brought the potential for new machines to be invented that ran on electricity and were driven by motors. At around the same time, the electrical

▲ Electricity has become an essential part of modern life.

communications industry was developing. The telegraph, telephone and radio revolutionised the lives of ordinary people at the start of the 1900s. In just 100 years, beliefs about electricity had changed – no longer a mysterious force, electricity was now the main energy source of modern civilisation.

Electricity didn't completely dominate the new era however. In the late 1800s, the internal combustion engine was developed and diesel and petrol engines (rather than electric motors) soon replaced steam engines for use in vehicles for road, water and air. This was primarily because crude oil was widely available and easier to carry onboard a vehicle than an electricity supply. To this day electrically-powered vehicles are relatively uncommon on the road. Instead, electricity is mainly used in locomotives and trams because electricity can be fed through the tracks upon which the railed vehicles travel, removing any need to carry fuel cells. The vehicles that are electrically powered tend to be those like golf buggies, which are quiet to drive but can never travel too far before needing to be recharged with electricity.

▲ This illustration shows Michael Faraday giving a lecture at the Royal Institution in London in the 1830s. Faraday's work brought many advances in the study of electricity and his lectures made science very popular amongst the general public.

▲ Trams are powered by electricity from tracks in the road or cables suspended above. Trams are common across Europe and are seen here at Rotonde station in Strasbourg, France.

Saving energy

Energy is a valuable commodity, so it makes sense to use it efficiently and economically. As technology improves and countries such as China and India begin to develop rapidly, we are using energy resources more than ever before. As well as looking for alternative energy sources that can reduce our reliance on fossil fuels, it is important that we try to reduce the amount of energy that we use in our daily lives.

SAVING ENERGY IN INDUSTRY

Government schemes are trying to encourage the industrial and manufacturing industries to save more energy. Some factories are buying efficient equipment that needs less energy to work. At the same time, factories are also looking at ways to reduce the amount of polluting gases that they release into the air so that the energy they use is less damaging to the environment.

Manufacturers and designers can also work to increase the efficiency of the devices that they make so that we use the least energy possible. For example, a car loses energy through friction between the tyres and the road, the friction between moving parts of the engine, air resistance and the waste coming from exhaust fumes. Most of this energy is lost as heat. Car manufacturers try to design cars to use energy more efficiently. To minimise the amount of friction, the moving parts of the engine need to be made very accurately and lubricated with oil, so that they move smoothly past each other. Air resistance can also be reduced by giving the car a smooth and streamlined shape, so that the air molecules slide around it. Car heaters are used to recycle the heat loss by fanning air currents over the engine and then pumping the warmed air into the car. This small-scale energy economy can make a big difference when you think of the number of cars that are currently on the road.

SAVING ENERGY IN THE HOME

Other examples of energy efficiency can be found in the home. Insulation is a very good way of preventing energy from escaping a home. Cavities in walls provide an air gap to lessen the conduction of energy and they often include layers of foam or glass wool insulation to reflect energy back into the home. The same materials are also found in loft spaces to prevent convection currents from carrying energy away. Double-glazing has a similar insulating effect by using a layer of partial vacuum between the panes of glass, which prevents the conduction of thermal energy. Insulation works in reverse too, so that unwanted heat is prevented from entering houses on hot days.

▲ Modern cars are designed to use the least energy possible, while maintaining a space that is practical to use.

DID YOU KNOW?

▶ Since 1996, wind-up radios have been widely used in Africa. The device, called the Freeplay radio, runs without batteries or electricity which are both scarce and expensive in many African countries. The Freeplay radio works using the stored energy from a spring. When a lever is cranked on the side of the radio, the energy is transferred to a spring inside the radio. The kinetic energy is stored as potential energy which can be slowly released. A generator inside the radio then converts the spring's energy into electrical energy. It takes just 60 turns of the crank to power the radio for about an hour.

▲ Insulating homes with fibreglass helps to save heat energy.

Supplementing homes with electrical energy from solar and wind energy units is now becoming a phenomenon of the modern age. These devices reduce the amount of energy that a house needs to take from the national supply of electricity that is generated by power stations. In turn, solar and wind power save on valuable reserves such as oil, coal and gas and produce less pollution for the environment.

Changing behavioural patterns is another good way to save on energy in the home. Just turning off the lights can make a big difference. In most homes, more than half of the energy used is for heating. You can save energy by turning the heating down slightly and wearing a jumper instead. Boilers that only heat your water when you need it are also a good way to save energy. Recycling materials, such as glass and plastic, can help too. Recycling uses less energy than making objects from new glass or plastic. If you recycle two glass bottles it saves the energy needed to boil enough water for five cups of tea!

▲ Many everyday items can be recycled to save energy.

TIME TRAVEL: INTO THE FUTURE

▶ In the coming years, hydrogen-powered vehicles may become more common on our streets. Instead of using a traditional combustion engine (that releases carbon dioxide and other dangerous pollutants into the air) hydrogen cars use a hydrogen fuel cell. The fuel cell combines hydrogen (stored in the vehicle) with oxygen from the air to form water, generating electricity and heat in the process. The electricity is used to run an engine that powers the wheels.

Energy is a vital part of our lives. Today we have a better understanding of the way that energy works and the way it can be changed from one form to another. Sometimes, energy is used in unusual ways to solve the problems that affected many generations before us. Energy is as much a part of our lives today as it was in the past, but we are lucky to have found new and exciting ways to use it.

THE POWER OF THE SEA

In places where rainfall is either unreliable or seasonal, farmers can have real problems watering their crops. Wherever possible, farmers use **irrigation** to make sure that water reaches their plants. This involves the diversion of water from nearby rivers or lakes along channels, which branch out to feed a row of plants. In the past, if irrigation was impossible in a certain area, farming was extremely difficult. However, in coastal regions it has now been discovered that seawater can be used as an energy source for irrigation. Cold seawater is pumped through a system of pipes that run close to the roots of the crop plants. The cold temperature causes water vapour in the air to condense on the pipes, so that the soil remains moist enough for the roots of the plants to absorb it.

It is also possible to acquire fresh water from seawater, so that it can be used for human and animal consumption. Two methods are currently available. The first is the process of distillation. Energy is used to heat seawater so that water vapour escapes into a chamber. The water vapour is then fed into a system of cooled pipes so that it condenses into fresh water. Adding energy and then removing it causes the water to lose its salt. The second method relies on the energy with which atoms are attracted to one another. Special atoms of plastic are used in seawater filters. These atoms attract the salt molecules, so that the water passes through as fresh water.

EXPANSION AND CONTRACTION

There are many situations in which people take advantage of the fact that materials expand when they heat up and contract when they cool down. Thermometers use expanding liquids to record temperatures. Mercury or alcohol is used to fill a bulb at the base of a glass thermometer. When the liquid warms up it expands and rises up a tube, which is marked to show temperatures relating to the body perhaps or the air temperature (see page 31).

▲ There is an abundance of saltwater in the oceans of our planet. Thanks to new energy techniques, seawater can now be used to produce fresh water for drinking or for irrigating crops.

◄ A source of heat energy accelerates the motion of molecules in the air so that they become less dense, helping this hot air balloon to rise.

Examples of expanding solids are seen in the metal tyres of old cartwheels and the hoops of wooden barrels. In both cases the iron is heated so that it expands and fits over the wheel or barrel. Water is then used to cool the iron, with the result that it contracts or shrinks to form a tight fit. Examples of expanding gas are seen in the hot air balloon and the **glider**. A hot air balloon is filled with hot air, which is lighter than the surrounding air, so that it rises. When the hot air cools, the balloon descends. A glider takes advantage of naturally rising convection currents of hot air, called thermals, which push beneath the wings and keep the glider airborne.

SPACE TRAVEL

It has recently been discovered that laser beams can be used as sources of energy for rockets and missiles. The technique uses a laser beam that is focused so that it shines upwards into a cone beneath the rocket. The intensity of the laser beam causes atoms in the cone to become overheated so that they explode. These explosions cause a downward force which propels the rocket upwards. This method can only be used for launching rockets because the laser beam needs to be constant, to keep the rocket moving. However, this exciting technology could save space rockets from having to carry the vast amounts of fuel they need to escape the Earth's atmosphere.

ELECTRICAL THINKING

Machines such as computers, calculators and word processors are electronic tools that enable us to do mental tasks very quickly – such as researching information, calculating sums and writing text. The modern world operates far more quickly than it did before the advent of electrical thinking. In a way, we have used energy to supplement the overall ability and skill of the human brain, because we cannot evolve quickly enough ourselves to match technological progress.

MANUFACTURING

Sources of energy can also be use to make other things. For example, oil can be refined and used to make products such as plastic, soap and even cosmetics. Chemicals and gases can be removed from natural gas and used to make washing powders, plastics and even medicines. Some fertilisers that farmers use to add goodness to the soil (to make their crops grow strong and healthy) are made with sulphur and nitrogen, which come from natural gas.

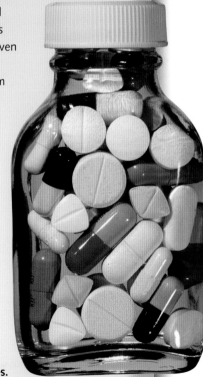

▶ Sources of energy can be used to make many products, such as medicines.

Glossary

ABSOLUTE ZERO – The temperature at which substances possess no heat energy (approximately -273°C or 0°K).

ACID RAIN – Rain that contains high levels of nitric or sulphuric acid. Acid rain forms when gases from industrial fuels combine with moisture in the atmosphere.

AIR CONDITIONER – A machine that uses a cooling mechanism to control the temperature in a warm room.

ATOM – The smallest piece of a pure chemical element, such as hydrogen.

BATTERY – A portable container which contains chemicals that can produce an electric charge.

CENTRAL HEATING – A system powered by oil, gas or electricity that can be used to warm water and the rooms of a property.

CHAIN REACTION – A series of reactions which cause further reactions to occur. Nuclear energy produces a chain reaction, for example.

COMBUSTION – The process of burning, caused by a rapid chemical reaction between two (or more) substances. Combustion produces heat and light energy.

COMPOUND – A substance consisting of two (or more) atoms.

CONDENSATION – When a substance changes from a gas to a liquid.

CONVECTION – The transfer of heat in a gas or a liquid, caused by a variation in densities.

ELECTRICITY – The movement of electrically-charged particles.

ELECTROMAGNETIC – Having both electrical and magnetic properties. Electromagnetic radiation (such as visible light) has electric and magnetic fields that vary simultaneously.

EQUATOR – An imaginary circle around the Earth, halfway between the North and South Poles.

EXOTHERMIC – A chemical reaction that releases heat energy.

ANSWERS

p19 Test yourself
(1) Kinetic energy, electrical energy, heat energy, light energy.
(2) Kinetic energy, electrical energy, heat energy.
(3) Kinetic energy, electrical energy, sound energy.
(4) Kinetic energy, chemical energy, heat energy, light energy.
(5) Kinetic energy, potential energy.

p24 Test yourself
Oil – made from the remains of prehistoric animals. It is burnt to provide heat energy that can be used in a power station to make electricity. Oil can also be refined to make petrol and diesel to power vehicles. Natural gas – made from the remains of prehistoric plants and animals. Natural gas is burnt to provide heat energy that can be used in a power station to make electricity. Natural gas can also be used in our homes for cooking and heating.

Coal – made from the remains of prehistoric plants. It is burnt to provide heat energy that can be used in a power station to make electricity. Coal can also be burnt directly in fire, to heat our homes for example.
Peat – made from the remains of plants. Peat is burnt in fires, to heat our homes, for example.

p26 Investigate
See illustration on p10.

FRACTIONAL DISTILLATION – A process that separates chemical substances by their varying boiling points. Crude oil is usually distilled using this process.

FREEZING POINT – The temperature at which a liquid turns into a solid. The freezing point of a substance is also its melting point.

FRICTION – A force that occurs when two (or more) materials rub together. Friction slows down movement and produces heat.

GLIDER – An aircraft without an engine that flies using rising currents of hot air.

GLOBAL WARMING – A sustained increase in the average temperature of the Earth's atmosphere which can cause climate change. Global warming is thought to be caused by the burning of fossil fuels.

GRAVITY – The force that pulls all materials together across space.

INCANDESCENT – A substance that emits light energy when it is heated.

IRRIGATION – The process of watering crops using artificial sources of water.

MAINS ELECTRICITY – A term to describe a national power supply that provides electricity to buildings, via power lines across the country.

MELTING POINT – The temperature at which a solid turns into a liquid. The melting point of a substance is also its freezing point.

MOLECULE – A particle made from two (or more) atoms or one (or more) elements.

NUCLEUS – The centre of an atom which is made up of protons and neutrons.

PHOTOSYNTHESIS – The process in green plants in which foods (mainly sugars) are made from carbon dioxide and water, using energy from the sunlight.

POLLUTION – Contamination of the environment as a result of human activities.

RADIATION – The transmission of energy through space. Heat energy from the Sun travels to the Earth as radiation, for example.

REPRODUCE – To produce offspring through sexual or asexual reproduction.

RESPIRATION – The process of releasing energy from food. Respiration needs the food we eat and the oxygen we breathe.

STATIC ELECTRICITY – An electrical charge that accumulates on an object when it is rubbed against another object. Static electricity is caused by a movement of electrons.

TIDE – The regular rise and fall of the surface of the oceans caused by the pull of the Sun and Moon.

Useful websites:
www.bbc.co.uk/schools
www.popsci.com
www.sciencenewsforkids.org
www.newscientist.com
www.howstuffworks.com

Index